The Delta Queen

THE DELTA QUEEN

Last of the Paddlewheel Palaces

By AUGUST PEREZ & ASSOCIATES
Myron Tassin, Editor

PELICAN PUBLISHING COMPANY
Gretna 1973

Manufactured in the United States of America
Designed by J. Barney McKee
Published by Pelican Publishing Company, Inc.
630 Burmaster Street, Gretna, Louisiana 70053

Library of Congress Cataloging in Publication data:

August Perez & Associates
  The Delta Queen: Last of the Paddlewheel Palaces.

  1. Delta Queen (Steamboat). I. Tassin, Myron, ed.

II. Title.

VM461.D4A9   386'.22'43   73-9567

ISBN 0-88289-008-5

Dedications

This photo essay is dedicated to the ladies and gentlemen of the United States Congress whose hands hold the future of the *Delta Queen*.

Royalties from this book are dedicated to support an annual group travel grant for deserving architecture students enrolled in the School of Environmental Design at Louisiana State University.

Contents

INTRODUCTION

Presently a film of dark smoke appears . . . instantly a Negro drayman, famous for his quick eye and prodigious voice, lifts up the cry, 'S-t-e-a-m-boat a-comin'!' . . . Drays, carts, men, boys, all go hurrying from many quarters to a common center, the wharf. Assembled there, the people fasten their eyes upon the coming boat as upon a wonder they are seeing for the first time.

—Mark Twain, *Life on the Mississippi*

Mark Twain, the most cynical of men, could wax lyrical over the coming of a steamboat on the river. Time has not diminished the thrill felt by young and old alike at the sight of a gleaming white paddle-wheeler, leaving a trail of churning water in her wake as her powerful engines bring her around the bend and toward the dock.

Steamboating was the dominant form of travel on the rivers of our nation for a fairly short time—about fifty years of the nineteenth century. But this mode of travel has come to stand as a symbol of the gracious, elegant past, particularly in the South.

Riverboat gamblers, stern captains, painted women, Natchez-under-the-Hill, Ol' Man River, the *Natchez* and the *Robert E. Lee*, crystal chandeliers, and mahogany bars—the visions conjured up by the magical word *steamboat* are many. Steamboating was a mode of transportation, certainly, and it was of great economic importance in its time. But more than that, it captured by its very nature the mood and life-style of its time.

Today there is only one overnight passenger steamboat on the inland waters of the United States. She is the *Delta Queen*, a sternwheeler imported from California in 1947, which has since logged more than a million miles of leisurely travel on the Mississippi River and its tributaries. Owned and operated by Greene Line Steamers, Inc., of Cincinnati, the *Queen* makes fifty to sixty cruises each year during her February to December season. She is 285 feet long, powered by two 1,000-horsepower steam engines, has a crew of seventy-five, and can accommodate some two hundred passengers.

Those are the facts about the *Queen*, but it is not the purpose of this volume merely to deal with facts. In words and pictures we hope to capture for you the mood, the feel of the era, of a cruise on the *Queen*, to tell you something of her history and the history of the rivers and towns she visits on her journeys.

We will also tell you of the importance of the continued existence of the *Queen* as an overnight riverboat.

After you have read this book, we sincerely hope that you will have a better understanding of what the continuation of the *Queen* means to those of us who value our tenuous links with the past.

Johnny Cash, better known for singing the praises of America's railroads, also has spoken of riverboats in general and the *Delta Queen* in particular. Here is how he put it:

"Our young nation built its towns on the banks of rivers, and down the rivers came burly men, bringing the necessities of life on crude flatboats and rafts.

"A half century later the rivers were teeming with scows, shantyboats, towboats and packets. They transported planters, merchants, soldiers, drovers, writers, missionaries, gamblers, and fancy women. And if it was action you were looking for, you'd head for the river.

"Only one paddlewheel steamboat is left on the American rivers. She's the *Delta Queen*, Port of Cincinnati. She's a big, beautiful white sternwheeler with shining brass fixtures, polished mahogany and elegant staircases. But don't let her shiny clean appearance fool you. She's beautiful, but she's tough.

"For a short while longer, the *Delta Queen* will paddle up and down the Ohio and Mississippi carrying modern Americans briefly back through the past.

"Again you'll hear the sparkle of the banjo and you'll almost feel the presence of Mark Twain, Huckleberry Finn, the Civil War guns, and the wild thumping heartbeat of past Americans.

"There ain't nothing like her, and never will be again. Take your hat off, Mister, you're seein' the passing of a great lady."

> *So long,* Delta Queen,
>
> *Cincinnati down to New Orleans*
>
> *When you go you'll take a lot of dreams,*
>
> *So long,* Delta Queen.

AUGUST PEREZ, JR.
AUGUST PEREZ, III

AN ANCESTRY OF BLUEBLOODS

The Mississippi is well worth reading about. It is not a commonplace river, but on the contrary is in all ways remarkable.

—Mark Twain, *Life on the Mississippi*

First there was the river. The brown, mile-wide Mississippi, running down to the Gulf of Mexico, past rocky bluffs in the North, and muddy, willow-lined banks in the South. Carrying the soil of a continent, it twists and turns like a giant serpent, leaving horseshoe lakes cut off from the main body of water, treacherous sandbars, and wooded islands.

Then there were the Indians. They found the river first a barrier and then a road as they traversed the central part of the continent searching for new hunting grounds and homelands. With the birchbark canoe on the upper waters near the Great Lakes, and with cottonwood dugouts and rafts on the broad lower waters, the Indians used the great river long before the first white man stood on its banks.

It was a Spaniard, Hernando de Soto, who, in 1542, discovered the great Father of Waters and claimed it for King Philip of Spain. De Soto died of fever on its banks and was buried in it by his men. More than a century would pass before other European explorers were to venture on its broad waters. Eventually the French pitted their skills and daring against the big river. Joliet and Marquette traveled the upper waters down to the Arkansas in 1673 and ventured the theory that the Mississippi flowed into the Gulf of Mexico.

But it remained for René Robert Cavalier, Sieur de la Salle, to reach the mouth of the river. In 1682 he took possession of the entire region drained by the river for his French king and queen, naming it Louisiana in their honor. Another century passed before the river became an important commercial artery for the youthful country. This time it was the keelboats, flatboats, and broadhorns floating down to New Orleans, manned by a rough and colorful breed of men, the kind who could describe themselves in this manner: "I'm the old original iron-jawed, brass-mounted, copper-bellied corpse-maker from the wilds of Arkansaw!" At first the keelboats would float downstream from the northern ports and unload at New Orleans. After the steamboat intruded on their world, they continued the downstream trip for a time, eventually selling their boats in New Orleans and riding back upstream on those of their competitors.

It was inevitable that the slow and unwieldly barges would give way to a swifter means of transportation, but it was not an overnight process. As the keelboatmen battled the muddy water, cursing its tricky currents and hidden snags, their fate was being sealed far to the east. John Fitch of Connecticut launched his steamboat on the Delaware in 1787, and that same year James Rumsey put his craft into the waters of the Potomac. The pioneering continued for several years with Robert Fulton in 1807 making the trip from New York to Albany on his famous *Clermont* in thirty-two hours and John Stevens taking his *Phoenix* to Philadelphia by sea in 1808.

But these developments did not yet affect travel on the Mississippi River. In 1811 Nicholas Roosevelt, an agent for Fulton and Robert Livingston, built the *New Orleans* at Pittsburgh. He set out down the Ohio with his wife amid predictions of disaster. Nine months later, in January, 1812, there was great excitement in New Orleans as the boat named for that city pulled up to its wharves, having survived breakdowns and an earthquake to complete a historic journey.

Fulton and Livingston, having obtained a monopoly contract for operation of steamboats on the Mississippi from New Orleans to Natchez, launched five boats in the years that followed Roosevelt's trip. But the deep-draft vessels were more steamships than steamboats, and it was not until 1816 that the first boat designed solely for Mississippi River travel appeared. She was the *Washington*, belonging to Henry Miller Shreve, engineer and inventor as well as boatman. His craft, propelled by a high-powered engine that could battle the mighty currents, was mounted on a shallow-draft, bargelike hull, with a tall second deck, and paddlewheels at the side.

His boat made the trip from New Orleans to Louisville in twenty-five days, a marvelous feat for its time. Shreve successfully fought the Fulton monopoly, and boats built along the lines of the *Washington* soon became common all along the Mississippi.

It was the steamboat that truly began the opening of the West to settlement, long before the railroads. Towns fortunate enough to be located on the rivers, especially the Mississippi, grew and prospered. In the twenty years from 1814 to 1834, steamboat arrivals in New Orleans increased from twenty to twelve hundred per year. That city especially benefited from cotton trade via steamboats, developing a port second only to New York and doubling its population in the decade of the 1830s. Memphis, St. Louis, Natchez, and other cities along the Mississippi also benefited from the steamboat boom.

The golden age of steamboating on the Mississippi lasted only fifty years, from 1820 to 1870. But in those years the "floating palaces" won for themselves a unique and revered place in American life. From Mark Twain's definitive account of life on the Mississippi to Jerome Kern's romantic *Showboat* to the contemporary rock saga *Proud Mary*, steamboats have been loved and revered by countless authors, poets, and songwriters.

They well deserve this praise, for they were amazing vessels, ornate with gingerbread carvings that made some call them "floating wedding cakes." They had lavish lounges rivaling the finest hotel lobbies of the time, fine bars, barber shops, menus containing seven soups and fifteen desserts, and even their own newspapers, printed to keep passengers informed of events during their voyages.

With names such as *J. M. White*, *New Orleans*, *America*, *Valley Queen*, *John Howard*, *Sultana*, *Belle of Memphis*, *Imperial*, *Silver Wave*, *Princess*, *Mayflower*, and, of course, *Natchez* and *Robert E. Lee*, the great boats ruled the river from St. Paul to Barataria, carrying cotton to New Orleans for export to Europe and a colorful group of passengers to various destinations.

The tall, stately vessels gleamed white in the southern sun as they churned through the muddy water with their twin paddlewheels making trails in the river and double smokestacks clouding the sky. The boats were majestic—as were the men who manned them—the captain, who ruled his boat like an autocrat; the skillful pilot, who knew every inch of the twisting river, every shoal, every snag; the oil-stained engineer, a master mechanic who could keep the high-pressure engines chugging away despite all manner of handicaps.

When the steamboat whistle sounded, townspeople rushed to the banks of the river. There were goods to be unloaded, more goods to be taken aboard, mail sacks to be handled, passengers to be met, others to be bidden farewell. If there was time (and there usually was in those less hurried times), there might be an impromptu concert by some of the hands on fiddle or harmonica, a forerunner of the elaborate showboats that brought entertainment to the river towns.

Gradually sternwheeled steamboats began to appear on the river and eventually outnumbered the sidewheelers. Somewhat plainer than the elaborate sidewheelers, the sternwheelers possessed the virtues of economy, simplicity, and ruggedness, especially in narrow and shallow streams where the sidewheelers would be vulnerable to damage. The boats were called packets if they served regular routes, but most of them would pull in wherever a signal from shore indicated that a passenger or cargo was waiting.

In 1853 the great boat *Eclipse* made the New Orleans to Louisville run in less than 4½ days, and it was widely believed that the steamboat represented the ultimate in fast, luxurious travel. But there was domestic turmoil on the wind, and soon the nation was engaged in a great Civil War. The steamboats were replaced by gunboats, and during the war the railroads were relied upon more and more for transportation.

After the war, the luxury packets made a brief comeback, climaxed in 1870 by the great race between the *Natchez* and the *Robert E. Lee*, won by the latter which reached St. Louis from New Orleans in three days, eighteen hours, and fourteen minutes.

Finally the railroads replaced the steamboats as major movers of goods and people. One by one the steamboats left the river, to be replaced by functional but unromantic towboats and barges.

As Harry Sinclair Drago notes in his book *The Steamboaters*, "We write songs and stories about them which, if they do nothing else, keep our memories of them green. But we cannot call them back."

Today, only the *Delta Queen* remains to give us a picture of life on the Mississippi during these long-vanished days and to "keep our memories green."

*It was a time when a man could perch on driftwood
and watch the world go by.*

They were built by a special breed of men who would not wait for rails to open the West and South to settlement.

They were christened after river towns . . .

After states . . .

For plantation owners . . .

And steamboating men.

Some were modest—small enough to ply narrow Louisiana bayous.

Others, like the J. M. White,
were lavish, luxurious floating palaces.

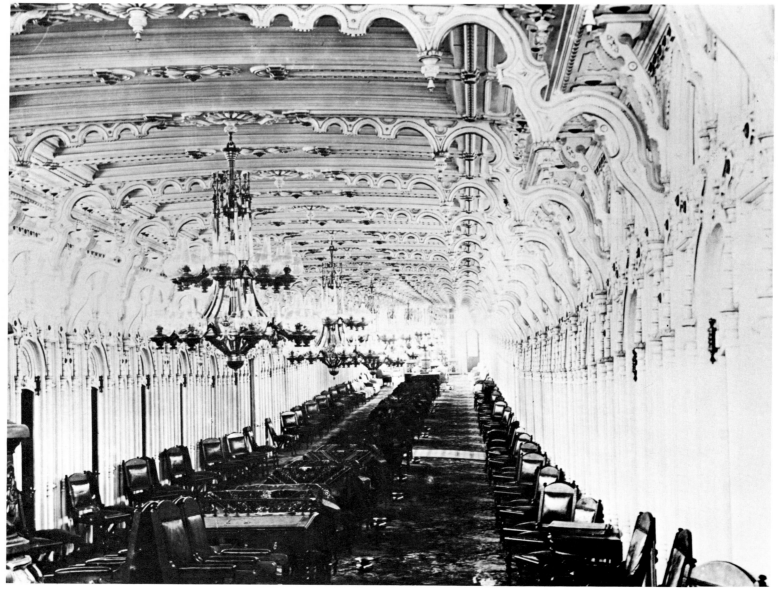

*Their paddlewheels moved goods and people up and down
the waterways of America's heartland.*

If cotton was king . . .

. . . steamboats crowned it so.

Shipped, in good order and well-conditioned, by Meyer Weis & Co on board the Steamboat called the R. E. Lee whereof Cannon is Master, now lying in the Port of New Orleans, and bound for Natchez being marked and numbered as in the margin; and are to be delivered in the like order and condition, at the Port of Natchez (the dangers of Navigation and Fire only excepted) unto Dryden Stockman or to his assigns, he or they paying Freight for the said

In Witness Whereof, The Master or Clerk of the said Steamboat hath affirmed to Three Bills of Lading, all of this tenor and date, one of which being accomplished, the others to stand void.

Dated in New Orleans, the 11 day of Dec 186 6

Stevens & Seymour, 93 & 96 Common Street, N. O.

MARKS.	ARTICLES.	
Farrar & Co Care Dryden Stockman Natchez	1 one case mdse 2 Two Bales do	Robert Oil

*Cargo ranged from needles and thread
to a deckload of juicy Calhoun County apples.*

. . . permeated the marrow of sportin' men's bones.

CAPT. T. P. LEATHER

CAPTAIN JOHN W. CANNON.

*A time when the ornate floating cakes attracted
big men and con men alike.*

Ice gorges, narrows, sandbars,

snags, shoals, exploding boilers . . .

none could deter the determined rivermen.

The vessels increased in number until ports such as New Orleans received up to twelve hundred arrivals a year . . . more than three a day.

They brought the stage and painted women to the crossroads of America . . .

*And calliope music to liven the sounds
of sleepy river haunts (the Magnolia, shown above,
was the first steamboat to have a calliope).*

*Their omnipotent captains
could eject an unruly passenger
on some barren riverbank
with the wave of his hand.*

They ferried trains where there were no bridges . . .

Served as lifelines when floods isolated their victims . . .

Stopped at plantations to pick up the season's harvest.

When the whistle sounded, frenzied activity followed as townspeople rushed to riverbanks.

In all sizes and shapes, they came and went for fifty years
before the golden age of steamboating
began to ebb . . .

One by one they left the rivers . . .

To be replaced by functional but unromantic towboats and barges . . .

And then there was one.

AN INTERNATIONAL MONARCH

When I was a boy, there was but one permanent ambition among my comrades in our village on the west bank of the Mississippi River. That was, to be a steamboatman.

—Mark Twain, *Life on the Mississippi*

The *Delta Queen* was born on a river, but not the Mississippi, or the Ohio, or the Missouri. It was on the River Clyde at Glasgow, Scotland, that her mighty steel hull was fabricated. Her machinery was also built in Scotland, at Dumbarton, and her wheel shafts and cranks were forged by the famous Krupp plant in Germany. But her four decks and her cabins were constructed by American shipbuilders.

In the early 1920s steamboating on American rivers was long past its prime. But it would become a new thing on the Sacramento River in California, between San Francisco and Sacramento. The bold men of the California Transportation Company were willing to bet $2 million that steamboating would again become popular.

The Scottish hulls for the *Queen* and her companion ship, the *Delta King* were barged to Stockton, California, where master shipbuilder Jim Burns, a tough Irishman, designed and built both vessels, using the finest oak, teak, mahogany, and Oregon cedar. The big stern-wheelers were designed to be as elaborate as the finest craft of the Mississippi River steamboat days—and perhaps more so.

From 1924 to 1926 Burns and his crews worked on the two boats, until, finally, they were ready for service.

From 1926 to World War II, the twin boats carried passengers on overnight trips on the Sacramento, with frequent excursions on the San Joaquin River to Stockton. The valley of the Sacramento is a delta, and the two vessels derived their names from this fact. The fertile land is protected by levees much like the sugar cane country along the Mississippi below New Orleans.

The vessels represented heroic efforts to recapture the lost past, but when hard times came in the 1930s, there was little extra money in most budgets for pleasure travels. The California Transportation Company was absorbed by River Lines, Inc., which soon docked the boats. Finally they were sold to Isbrandtsen Steamship Line, which planned to use them on the Mississippi River. The company boxed up the *Delta King*, and planned to sail the vessel down the coasts of California, Mexico and Central America, through the Panama Canal, and across the Gulf of Mexico to New Orleans. It was necessary to box up the boat to keep the high ocean waves from sweeping through the superstructure and shoring was necessary to brace the relatively fragile craft against the buffeting she was sure to receive in open waters.

But the *King* never got past the Golden Gate Bridge. The Japanese attacked Pearl Harbor, and the U.S. Navy took over the two boats. Painted drab gray, the former pleasure craft were used for serious duties during the war, ferrying troops to and from ocean vessels in San Francisco Bay and taking wounded men from ships to hospitals.

In 1946 the navy offered the vessels at auction. The *King* was sold for $60,000 to an Asian firm. The craft was assumed to be seaworthy but was never used and is still docked in California.

Tom Greene of Greene Line Steamers, Cincinnati, purchased the *Queen* for $46,000. His was the only bid received. During World War II, the family-owned firm had successfully operated the passenger steamboat *Gordon C. Greene* on the Ohio and Mississippi, and Tom wanted a larger boat.

After the purchase, Greene tackled the problem of getting the river craft to the Mississippi. The *Queen* was taken to a shipyard in Antioch, California, where she was braced and boxed to become a seaworthy, if ungainly, craft.

While the *Queen* was being readied for her ocean voyage, her builder, the eighty-four-year-old Irishman Jim Burns, came to visit her for the last time. Asked how long he thought the *Queen* would last, he replied promptly: "She will last Captain Greene through his lifetime and someone after him."

Finally, in the spring of 1947, the boat was ready to travel. Called a "seagoing barge" on her inspection certificate, she was covered with unpainted wood and one observer described her as resembling "a huge piano box."

With the tugboat *Osage* hauling her along, the voyage began. After briefly running aground on a mud flat at the start of the journey, the *Queen* set out for the sea. She left San Francisco on April 19 and arrived in New Orleans one month later, safe and sound, having weathered ocean squalls and passed through the Panama Canal without incident.

At the end of her trip, the *Queen* bore the flag of each nation she had passed—Mexico, Guatemala, San Salvador, Honduras, Nicaragua, Costa Rica, and Panama—in addition to her American flag.

But the boat was still a long way from being ready for passengers. She had to be refinished and restored as a pleasure craft after years as a utilitarian wartime ferry. She was taken to Pittsburgh in August and completely overhauled.

The *Queen* did not leave Pittsburgh until February, 1948. As one observer remarked: "The *Delta Queen* went to the shipyard very much of a question mark, and she emerged every inch a steamboat." On June 30, 1948, the *Delta Queen* made a trip to Cairo, Illinois, inaugurating its service as a river pleasure boat.

Today the vessel remains within the borders of the United States, making more than fifty trips each year, along the banks of seventeen states and touching more than a hundred river towns.

She has come a long way, but her passengers—from the elderly couple relaxing in the quiet elegance of her stained-glass observation lounge to the youthful honeymooners strolling her decks to view the scenic river—are delighted that Tom Greene had his dream of a big steamboat on the Mississippi and possessed the resources and determination to make that dream come true.

Jim Burns's prediction that the *Delta Queen* would outlast her owner was not long in being fulfilled, for in 1950, only two years after her restoration, Tom Greene died at the age of forty-six.

His premature death left his widow, Mrs. Letha C. Greene, at the helm of Greene Line Steamers. She was the last of the Greene family and the responsibility of the traditional family business fell directly upon her.

Declining freight revenues, coupled with a changing economy, forced the sale of the steamers *Evergreene*, *Chris*, *Tom*, and *Gordon*, the last of what once was a fleet of twenty-eight Greene Line packet and passenger steamboats. This trend continued for the eight years following Tom Greene's death. Company profits fell to such a low level by 1958 that the last of the Greene Line vessels, the stately *Delta Queen*, was on the auction block.

But just as the California steamboat *Delta Queen* had preserved passenger service on the inland waters, so it was that another California native, Richard Simonton, preserved steamboating by offering the financial backing and management capabilities to permit the last of the great riverboats to continue flying the Greene Line flag.

Simonton's timely appearance along with his able associate, William "Bill" Muster, who today is president of Greene Line, initiated a total restructuring of the company. By the 1960s, the operation of the *Delta Queen* bore little resemblance to its past. Proper maintenance and the long-neglected preservation work on the then thirty-four-year-old vessel was under way. Sound budgeting of financial resources permitted this work to continue as an on-going project. After all, although the *Delta Queen* was only in her mid-thirties, it was typical of steamboats in their heyday to last only twenty to twenty-five years. The *Delta Queen* had become an antique, deserving the care and consideration that a Chippendale or Louis XIV piece of furniture deserved.

The new Simonton-Muster leadership brought along changes in the vessel's operation, and more importantly, her public image. Slowly, national attention began to focus upon the last of the overnight steamboats, and this brought new revenues to the company. All these factors combined to make the *Delta Queen* an unqualified success by the mid-sixties. In fact, by this time, reservations aboard the *Delta Queen* were becoming difficult to obtain. For the first time, potential "steamboaters" often had to get on the waiting list, hoping for a cancellation and an opportunity to ride the *Delta Queen*.

Increased demand for passage brought with it hopes for rebuilding the Greene Line fleet. Plans were begun in 1965 to build a new riverboat. But despite the renewed success of the *Delta Queen,* the comparatively small Greene Line could not afford, nor did it have the expertise, to make the dream of a new fleet come true.

In 1969, after numerous attempts to build a new vessel, the owners of Greene Line sold the company to Overseas National Airways (ONA), an airline offering overseas charter service. ONA had the financial clout to carry out the dream; however, the technology needed to build a new sternwheel riverboat presented more financial and technological problems than anticipated, thus leaving the dream, at least temporarily, in limbo. Odd it is that the technology available to land men on the surface of the moon could not easily build a riverboat as was done when modern science was in its infancy.

The hopes for a new boat, however, are worthwhile only as long as the flagship *Delta Queen* exists, for she is the last and best of her kind. Without her, a new vessel would be of little significance.

So, the *Delta Queen* continues to operate, escorting the second half of the twentieth century into another chapter of unqualified success. Demand for passage continues to grow—passengers waiting for a chance to return to the 1870s, to ride a time machine traveling just six miles per hour, to experience what was once a most important factor in the early growth of the American West. Passengers strolling her decks are glad that Tom Greene had his steamboat dream, that Richard Simonton and Bill Muster appeared as the vessel literally was about to fall apart, that Captain Ernest Wagner, master of the *Delta Queen*, and a pretty young lady general manager, Betty Blake, are entwined in the determination and love of a common cause—the *Delta Queen.*

Who is the Delta Queen?

The monarch's steel hull was fabricated in Scotland,
her wheel shafts and cranks in Germany,
and her decks and cabins in America.

She and her brother, the Delta King *(right),*
served Californians until hard times of the 1930s docked them both.

*In 1947, boarded up and looking like "a huge piano box,"
she came through the Panama Canal to middle America.*

Today, the lady presents ''the sparkle of the banjo . . .
the presence of Mark Twain, Huck Finn . . .''

She is a genteel and gracious hostess . . .

Conducive to enjoyment of the good life.

She is communion with the wonders of nature.

Planned regression.

A chapel where solemn vows are exchanged.

She relaxes inhibitions . . .

Attracts a dedicated following . . .

Upholds the racing tradition.

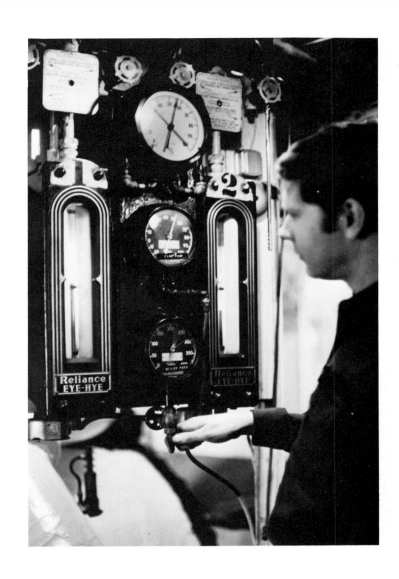

She is meticulously maintained . . .

Professionally operated.

*She brings "the wild
thumping heartbeat
of past Americans"
to fifteen cities . . .*

Cities like New Orleans, the Paris of America . . .

Memphis, home of the blues . . .

St. Louis, gateway to the West . . .

The Queen's *home port, Cincinnati* . . .

Mark Twain's boyhood home, Hannibal, Missouri . . .

Cave-in-Rock, Illinois, where pirates robbed steamboats.

Like a proud ghost, she churns slowly
through the twentieth century.

AFFAIR WITH KING JAZZ

After twenty-one years' absence I felt a very strong desire to see the river again, and the steamboats, and such of the boys as might be left; so I resolved to go out there.

—Mark Twain, *Life on the Mississippi*

THE FIRST EVENING

I have always been fascinated by the big river that curves around New Orleans and gave it the name "Crescent City." But I have thus far viewed it only from levees or wharves, from the tops of tall bridges or, more closely, from a ferry or local excursion boat.

Now, on this December day, my dream is to come true: a trip to Memphis from New Orleans aboard the sumptuous sternwheeler *Delta Queen*. The *Queen* is waiting for me at the foot of Toulouse Street in New Orleans' French Quarter, standing white and majestic on the brown water.

This cruise will be even more festive than usual; it is to be a jazz cruise, with concerts by noted jazz groups each day, mint julep parties, calliope music, oldtime vaudeville, and numerous jam sessions topped off with jazz "balls" in both Vicksburg and Memphis.

It is to be a historic voyage, for jazz has not been heard on the river since the 1920s when passenger boats regularly plied the muddy waters. It was on vessels much like the *Delta Queen* that New Orleans jazz bands first brought their unique, happy music up the river to Chicago, from where it spread out to the world.

Now there remains only the *Queen*, the last of her kind, waiting for me to board her and to be transported back to the leisurely living of the past.

The Olympia Brass Band is playing for the *Queen*'s departure. I quickly deposit my belongings in my cabin and hurry out to the foredeck for the party. As the band pauses, I note the gay music of a steam calliope being played by the *Queen*'s multi-talented interlocutor, Vic Tooker. At the appointed departure time, the *Queen*'s brass bell clangs a warning that all visitors must go ashore. With the Olympia Band playing "Didn't He Ramble," we ease silently away from the dock. The *Queen*'s ride is so smooth, there is almost no sensation of being afloat. There will be no seasick passengers here.

Dinner is served in the spacious Orleans Room, the *Queen*'s largest entertainment area. The buffet includes roast beef and a salad of crabmeat with all the trimmings. Later, there is a musical show featuring Vic Tooker and his parents who are former vaudevillians. The vessel's officers are introduced to us. Then, hostess Mariam Edgar demonstrates the use of the vest-type life jacket while Vic clowns with one in the background—an extremely effective demonstration.

Cajun raconteur Justin Wilson now gives his hilarious monologue and he is followed by two jazz bands: Bert Peck with his Kings of Dixieland and the Louisiana Jazz Club All-Stars. After the jazz session, a late snack buffet is wheeled in, and then we have an hour of dancing. The jazz musicians then get together for an informal jam session which lasts until 2:00 A.M.

Later I chat with Steve, bartender in the Mark Twain Lounge which is just aft from the Orleans Room. He is in school studying to be an architect, and works on the *Queen* only in alternate years. He knows it will take longer to finish school this way, but he's having fun aboard the *Queen* and at the same time financing his education. Many of the employees of the *Queen* are college students, he tells me. Since there's no occasion for them to spend money aboard the ship, they are able to save most of their pay for tuition and expenses.

My stateroom is not one of the more costly, but my bunk is wide and comfortable with a reading light above it. Lying in bed, tired after this eventful day, I hear the faint engine noises below—the surge of steam into the *Queen*'s two huge pistons, a steady rhythm, neither loud nor metallic, audible but very good for sleeping.

BATON ROUGE BOUND

Next morning is foggy, the temperature mild. A porter sounds reveille on a set of chimes, and I arise for a hearty breakfast of eggs and sausage. Breakfast snacks are served in the Texas Lounge until 10 A.M., we are told. By midmorning, the fog has still not lifted; neither bank of the river is visible. But the *Queen* steams ahead safely, guided by her radar.

Despite the weather, Miriam organizes a kite-flying contest. We assemble the kites ourselves. They are all printed with "Delta Queen."

I tour the ship and observe the spacious air-conditioned cabins on the third and fourth decks, the ornate carved wood, polished brass, and muted colors of the lobbies, and the ambient Old World elegance of the vessel.

Vic Tooker gives us a calliope demonstration, informing us that the *Queen*'s calliope dates from 1890. He plays the "Eli Greene Cake Walk," dedicated to the founder of Greene Lines, owner of the *Queen*. He announces that ".Vox Calliopus" certificates will be awarded to all who, in the captain's judgment, can play a recognizable tune on the calliope. Most participants manage "Chopsticks" or the "Dragnet" theme, and we are told that our certificates will be presented to us formally at dinner that evening.

The crew stages a lifeboat drill, donning life jackets and preparing the boats for lowering. The drill is a regular event at the beginning of each cruise. The crew is quiet and efficient in its work; they point out that, in addition to the lifeboats, there are automatically inflatable rafts located everywhere on the *Queen*'s weatherdecks. We remark later over coffee on the friendliness of both the crew and the officers.

The fog lifts shortly before noon, and I can now see the willows along the banks of the lower Mississippi.

At lunch there is ham and turkey, marinade, shrimp salad, and a desert of coconut cream pie. We are told that we should walk eleven turns around the deck each day for exercise; after finishing the pie, it seems to me like a good idea.

That afternoon, the captain gives a short dissertation on navigation and points of interest along the river. Later, a press conference is held to discuss the jazz cruise with the media people on board. Soon, at Baton Rouge, we pass under the big bridge which goes directly over that city's busy port to the west bank of the river. We watch as a Japanese ship is being filled with grain at an elevator. Other ships are being loaded at the cargo docks near us. The sailors on these ships and the longshoremen on the docks wave at us as we steam by, and we are glad to know that the *Queen* is a welcome sight even to those who work on the river daily.

We tie up at Baton Rouge and lower our gangway. We are berthed only a short distance from the towering Louisiana State Capitol, a skyscraper built in an earlier era by Huey Long. Visitors are invited on board and the jazz bands play for them at a short reception. The *Queen*, in the meantime, is taking on fuel from a barge on her port side.

The sun is just setting over the west bank of the river as we glide away from our mooring at Baton Rouge. One of our passengers went ashore while we were there and returned with a newspaper. Reading it, I am reminded that here on the river there is no need for newspapers, television sets, radios, or telephones; one is overtaken by the feeling that he is in a long-gone era—an era with no necessity or desire for instant news. I put the paper down and gaze instead at the glorious sunset in hues of red, orange, and purple. I take a deep breath of the cool, moist river air. Life is indeed good, I decide.

After dinner that night (steak or catfish, and blueberry pie à la mode) the jazz bands give another performance, this one better than last night's—more relaxed, loose, and happy, the way good jazz should be played.

Curiosity prompts me to ask the bartender in the Texas Lounge how that room got its name. He tells me, in the steamboat tradition, it is so named because it is the largest lounge on the largest deck of the vessel and has the best view of the river. He tells me further that the *Queen* can clip along at ten miles per hour going downstream with a good tailwind, and usually makes about five miles per hour going upstream. He explains that riverboat people calculate in miles instead of knots since all their charts and navigation aids are measured in this way.

Tonight I met "Captain Betty"—Miss Betty Blake, vice-president of Greene Lines, an attractive young lady who will be queen of our jazz ball in Memphis.

The night ends with another jam session, lasting later than the one the night before. Strains of "The Saints" and "Muskrat Ramble" are going through my head as I finally hit my bunk in the early morning hours.

FROM NATCHEZ TO VICKSBURG

Today opened with a party in the Texas Lounge, featuring Vic Tooker and his talented parents performing on a variety of instruments. Where else could I have started the day in this manner?

This morning I met the youthful organist, Pete Eveland, who has been playing at mealtimes. He is a seminarian at a small school in Cincinnati. He took off from his studies to join this cruise and must make up his school work when he returns.

Lunch is ample and delicious—tuna salad, corned beef and cabbage, blackberry pie. Afterwards, I lean against the weatherdeck rail for a while, noticing that the battures and willows of south Louisiana are yielding to piney woods as we proceed north into Mississippi. A sailboat passes piloted by two young girls; they smile and wave at us, appearing to be bound for adventure on the river as carefree as Huck Finn.

In a chat with Kenny, our chief engineer, I learn that the *Queen* has two generating systems to provide 110-volt AC power. One of the systems is powered by steam, the other by a diesel engine; they are used alternately so that the one not in use can be serviced.

Charlie Booty, "the Professor," is the *Queen's* ragtime pianist-in-residence. From St. Louis, he is regarded as one of the best around. A few moments of listening to him practice for tonight's performance is enough to convince me.

Late this afternoon we arrived at Natchez, but docked at Vidalia, on the Louisiana side of the river. The across-water sight of Natchez, this fine old city sitting on its high bluffs, is always memorable, but from the deck of the *Queen* it is majestic. There is little left now of the once-notorious Natchez-under-the-Hill; just a few rundown brick buildings winding up the bluff.

The mayor of Natchez and a party of city officials meet us for a short reception. The Kings of Dixieland give a half-hour concert for the visitors. Then we leave for Vicksburg, and I settle down to write some cards to the folks back home. The *Queen* has its own postmark, and all stamps will be cancelled with the date and legend, "*Delta Queen*, U.S. Postal Contract Station, Steamboat Mail."

Vic Tooker.

The food continues to be excellent. This evening I had lamb chops. I note that tonight's show has generated a party mood. One gentleman gets up during a spirited jazz number and does his own impromptu dance. He said, "I just couldn't have lived with myself if I didn't just cut loose at least once." Well, it's that kind of music.

Then there was an old-fashioned "Paul Jones" dance, where the partners change during the stop-and-start music. Couples not changing on cue were eliminated, and the final couple still dancing was awarded a prize. A jam session again followed the dancing. The musicians, I learn, are mostly professionals, but a few are business or professional men who join the musical groups as a hobby. They're all first-rate jazzmen.

Tonight I have a chance to talk with Vic Tooker. He wears an officer's uniform with "Interlocutor" emblazoned in gold on his cap. He says there are two record albums sponsored by the *Queen*, one featuring himself and his parents doing riverboat musical numbers; the other, called "Sounds of the *Delta Queen*," captures such sounds as the whistles, bells, and engine room, of the vessel. Writer Bern Keating, I learn, has done a fine book on the Mississippi River for *National Geographic*, which features a color picture of the *Queen* on its cover. I resolve to pick up these items as soon as possible.

Our captain, "Big Ernie" Wagner, looks as if he just stepped off a turn-of-the century packet. He stands over six feet, six inches, with a rugged, tanned face, deep voice, and ready smile. But I am told he can be tough as nails when the occasion calls for it, and he does a good job of handling his seventy-five-man crew. A qualified master on both the Mississippi and Ohio rivers, he inspires confidence in all of us.

I also meet Bill Muster, president of Greene Lines of Cincinnati.

Again the steady rhythm of the *Queen*'s engine is my lullaby as we steam through the foggy night toward the bluffs of Vicksburg.

THE JAZZ BALL

Over coffee and eggs this morning, I realize that except for my single glance at one newspaper in Baton Rouge, I haven't heard or seen any news of the outside world in nearly three days. And I like it! It's cool and clear this morning; a stroll around the deck is invigorating.

We arrive at Vicksburg before noon, turning off the Mississippi to enter the Yazoo River and tying up at the Port of Yazoo which lies at the foot of Vicksburg's main street. Unlike the Baton Rouge port, there are no oceangoing ships here. There are, however, a great many barges and towboats. The *Sprague*, which is the only other stern-wheeler remaining on the river, is tied up just ahead of us. She is now permanently moored and is used as a museum and theater.

There are no levees as such at Vicksburg. The city is built on high bluffs, and its streets fall abruptly to the river from the city above. There is a vertical concrete buttress about thiry-five feet high built at the foot of the bluffs, evidently to keep the river from eating away at the soil. We are moored to this buttress with hawsers, and the shallow water permits us to get within about ten yards of the shore. Various heights of previous flood stages are recorded in paint on the buttress.

A number of pleasure boats mill around the *Queen* this morning, exchanging greetings with us. A bumboat calls to sell us items without charging state tax; we are, after all, on the "navigable waters of the United States."

I note that the gangway of the *Queen* is carpeted but wide enough for Captain Wagner to drive his Volkswagen ashore at the *Queen*'s several stops. I had seen the car on the foredeck and wondered about it. Today, however, he surprised me by breaking out a motorcycle which he will ride up the steep hill and into town. Ellyna Tatum, a jazz singer on the tour, hitches a ride on the back of it and screams all the way up the bluff as Big Ernie floorboards the machine and roars off.

There are news reporters aboard representing both the New York *Times* and the *National Observer*. There are also some free-lance journalists and photographers. They are fascinated with the oldtime jazz musicians on the trip and undoubtedly will have more material than they can ever use what with the quaintness of the musicians and the *Queen* herself.

The bands play a fine concert for a delegation from Vicksburg which visits us. As usual, "When the Saints Go Marching in" is the favorite. Then all of us sit down to a lunch of tiny boiled shrimp with horseradish sauce and more of that blueberry pie which is now destroying what waistline I formerly had. A few more turns around the deck will be needed to walk this off.

At the afternoon concert, I sit with our hostess, Mariam Edgar, born and raised in the Ohio River town of Marietta. I discover that she has a master's degree in speech and was a hostess on an ocean liner before joining the *Queen*'s staff.

The ball is held at the Vicksburg auditorium. A local jazz group opens

the program, followed by Justin Wilson's Cajun humor, then by Vic
Tooker and his parents. Danny Barker's Louisiana Jazz Club All-Stars
follow Vic, accompanying singer Tatum and jazz dancer Darreil John-
son. Captain Wagner and Miss Blake are then crowned king and queen
of the ball, with Bert Peck's Kings of Dixieland playing for dancing
after the coronation ceremony.

The big auditorium is ringing with the sounds of real Dixieland jazz.
It is difficult to believe that the hour is so late when the last number
is played. It's been a great night, but all of us are tired from the dancing
and partying. When we return to the *Queen* in the early morning hours,
we're grateful to find that the chef has set out a sandwich buffet.

CRUISING UP THE RIVER

Next morning while more visitors are touring the *Queen*, I lounge on
the deck and scan the Vicksburg skyline. There is a high-rise structure
abuilding downtown. A grain elevator with about fifteen storage silos
lies aft of us. Again today there is a good deal of barge traffic. In
addition to its busy port, Vicksburg is regional headquarters for the
Army Corps of Engineers. I conclude that the city's ties with the river
are deep and important.

The *Queen*'s throaty brass bell warns all visitors ashore as we prepare
to cast off for Memphis, our next and final stop. To reverse her direction
on the Yazoo and return to the Mississippi, the *Queen* must make a
180-degree turn, which she does with only a foot or two to spare on
each side. As we pass the *Sprague*, I notice that her sternwheel is
much larger than ours, reaching as high as our third deck. The vessel
itself is only a little larger than the *Queen*, but she was built to be a
workboat rather than a pleasure vessel and thus needed the extra
power.

By high noon we are back on the big Mississippi, enjoying turkey
salad and short ribs while listening to Pete Eveland play the organ.
I chat with Captain Jim Blum, the *Queen*'s young first mate and a licensed river pilot. He gives me some interesting facts about the *Queen*
—285 feet from stem to stern, first put into service on the West Coast,
then shipped to the Mississippi through the Panama Canal. It's quite
a story . . .

The afternoon is a quiet one, which I need after our night in Vicksburg. Dinner this evening is hearty: veal cordon bleu or liver with
onions and for dessert strawberry shortcake. Bert Peck plays piano
during the meal after which we have some more fine jazz music and
other entertainment capped by a jam session which brings out the
hard-core jazz passengers and lasts until early in the morning. The
musicians say that this kind of audience enthusiasm makes them play
"over their heads." Be that as it may, this is the best session yet.

In my bunk, I realize that while we passengers are partying and
sleeping (more of the former than the latter on this cruise), the crew
of the *Queen* is on duty in the pilot house, the engine room, and at
lookout stations. In the passenger area likewise, a crewman makes
rounds every twenty minutes during the night. I learn this from Mariam
Edgar, who tells me also that the *Queen*'s dance floor is the same one
installed when the vessel was first built in 1926. It has endured many
a happy evening, not to mention several on this cruise.

Tonight a few more of the passengers get up and stage impromptu dances for us, so carried away are they with the good-time sounds of Dixieland jazz.

ON TOWARD MEMPHIS

This morning is hazy with a moderate temperature. At breakfast, the pancakes and syrup are delicious; I barely have time to recover from them with a walk on deck before a Bloody Mary party starts up in the Texas Lounge. The Jazz Club All-Stars are playing there, and I marvel at the stamina of these musicians, many of whom are quite elderly. At this party there develops a rapport between the band and the audience such as happens only on rare occasions. The audience response is overwhelming, and this in turn spurs the band on to greater and greater heights. We wind up strutting single file around the lounge, ending with people who barely knew each other just a few days ago shaking hands, kissing, and embracing each other from the sheer joy of the event. It is a platonic session. During the party we pass many tows of barges; I know that if any of their crews hear us, they certainly would be tempted to swim over and join the fun.

Resting after the party, I continue my talk with Jim Blum, our first mate. He tells me that not only is the *Queen* 285 feet long, but she is 58 feet wide and steered by six rudders. She is powered by two water-tube boilers which burn Bunker-C fuel when it can be obtained and diesel fuel at other times. Fuel consumption is 250 gallons per hour, a bit more than my Volkswagen. I watched a fuel transfer this morning from a fuel barge propelled by a towboat at our port side. We top off the tanks with fuel and potable water at every stop. The water is taken only from approved municipal water supplies. Jim says that the *Queen* is licensed to carry 192 passengers; about 125 plus the entertainers are aboard for this December jazz cruise.

I run across Danny Barker in the aft lobby playing guitar for a group of ladies, who are staging a singalong. There's no lack of music on this trip.

Tonight we will all be guests at the Captain's dinner. This will be the last evening meal we will have aboard the *Queen* since another jazz ball is slated for Memphis the following night. At this dinner, all the officers are neatly attired in blue uniforms. It is an impressive affair with champagne furnished by the *Queen*'s management; it is marred only by the knowledge that this will be our last full night aboard.

Captain Wagner thanks us for being such good passengers, and Franklin Myles, our chief steward, says that in all his years aboard the *Queen*, he's never seen nicer folks. The chef outdoes himself, giving us a choice of prime rib of beef or Dover sole. We are each given a souvenir menu engraved with a likeness of the *Queen* and a short history of her. Pete Eveland plays the organ after supper as the room is rearranged into nightclub style. The All-Stars band opens the show, followed by Justin Wilson and a musical production called "The Show That Killed Vaudeville." It's a hilarious collection of songs, jokes, and skits. It amazes me that these groups have presented a different show each night of our cruise, never repeating any material. Tonight we're in an especially festive mood, and the Kings of Dixieland present some rousing music, first for listening and then for dancing before winding up at midnight.

Over a postshow drink, Danny Barker discusses jazz with one of the passengers. When the discussion turns to who "invented" jazz he remarks intimately, "Man, you can't invent jazz like you do a machine; it's a folk art and can't be invented any more than you can invent red beans and rice."

Jim Blum joins me, and says we are steaming against a strong downstream current plus a headwind, both of which are slowing us down. All last night, he says, we followed a towboat equipped with a depth finder so that we could "straighten out" the bends in the river rather than follow the channel markers.

The conversation turns to "quilling." On our first night out of New Orleans, I had been awakened by the *Queen*'s steam whistle making a familiar sound. After fully awakening, I realized someone in the pilothouse was deliberately using the whistle to "quill," to make a mournful wail by opening its valve to intermediate positions rather than simply to "On" or "Off." This was a practice of the oldtime steam railroaders of my boyhood and always instilled in me feelings of loneliness and "blues in the night." Some of the railroad "quillers" had been so distinctive that their call was as recognizable as their signature. Wondering who our steamboat "quiller" was, I noticed tonight that Jim wears a brass belt buckle engraved with a steam locomotive. More conversation reveals that he comes from a railroad family in Cincinnati and that his hobby is steam railroad lore. He now admits that he "quills" whenever he is within whistle-distance of a craft he knows.

This night the sad wail of the whistle is the last thing I hear before I fall asleep.

THE MEMPHIS BLUES

Today dawns warm and hazy. Our plans are to cruise steadily toward Memphis and to tie up at the foot of famous Beale Street in time to go ashore from there to the big jazz ball scheduled for tonight.

By midmorning we learn that our plans have gone awry and that we must put in at Helena, Arkansas, and travel by bus to Memphis if we are to arrive in time for the ball. There have been torrential rains in this area, and the river is high, making currents fast and boat travel slow. These rains, I discover, are the reason we were unable to reach Memphis on time. We are all sad to leave the *Queen* prematurely, but we board the buses and take off across the water-soaked highways toward Memphis.

We arrive at the Holiday Inn Rivermont in Memphis where the jazz ball is to be held and are assigned rooms where we can relax before the big event.

Despite our adversity, the ball really is a ball. Abe Franklin's band, a local group, opens the show. Abe plays a relaxed jazz trumpet, and has a good rhythm section with him. The Kings of Dixieland follow and the thousand or so people at the ball respond appropriately. The Kings have Bert Peck on vibes, Jim LaRocca on trumpet, and Bill Crais on trombone. "Mack the Knife" is a popular number.

Danny Barker and the Louisiana Jazz Club All-Stars follow and are replaced by the Tookers, Justin Wilson, and ragtime pianist Charlie Booty in that order. Then the Kings come back to play for dancing. It is past midnight when we leave, and we find ourselves in the middle of a sudden icestorm. Making our way toward the *Queen* through the sleet and freezing rain we discover that she won't be in to Beale Street until

2 A.M. We wait on a barge equipped as a waiting room, out of the freezing rain. Getting on board the *Queen* to round up our belongings, we learn that it is nearly impossible to get a cabdriver to come down the now-glazed cobblestones to the river. We settle down for one more night (actually only a few morning hours) aboard the *Queen*. After dozing for a while, then sipping the *Queen*'s black coffee for a longer while, I finally find a cabdriver reckless enough to come after us. I will return to New Orleans by plane.

At the crowded Memphis airport waiting for the morning flight to New Orleans I reflect on how fast, and efficient—but dull—our modern modes of travel have become. The trip down to New Orleans from Memphis will be quick, painless, and utterly forgettable. But, ah, the trip from New Orleans to Memphis; it will never be forgotten by any of us who made it.

We left the old girl, the *Queen*, there on the river, tied against a strong current, with sleet coming down to glaze her decks. But she still looked queenly, rising high and handsome out of the choppy brown water. I look at the sleek silver jet on the runway in front of me. Sure, it's faster. But how I wish I could be cruising back to New Orleans on the *Delta Queen*.

Our captain, "Big Ernie" Wagner.

Well, hello Delta.

Yes, Hello Delta.

It's so nice to have you back where you belong.

You're looking swell, Delta.

I can tell, Delta.

You're still blowing.

You're still glowing.

I feel the room swaying, while the band's playing . . .

One of those ole steamboat tunes from way back when.

Golly, gee, fellows, find her an empty knee, fellows!

Delta, please never go away.   *Delta, please never go away . . .* *

EPILOGUE

Mississippi steamboating was born about 1812; at the end of thirty years it had grown to mighty proportions; and in less than thirty more it was dead! A strangely short life for so majestic a creature.

—Mark Twain, *Life on the Mississippi*

But Mississippi steamboating is not quite dead. As long as the *Delta Queen*'s red paddlewheel turns, her gay calliope plays, and her mournful whistle fills the foggy night with sound, there will be steamboating on the river.

With so much in modern life that is imitative, shoddy, uninspiring, this one grand reminder of our past must not be laid to rest.

That was the feeling of a great number of Americans, including many who had never even seen the *Queen*, when they learned that this grand old lady was included in the provisions of the "Safety at Sea Law" of 1966. The law was designed to protect American citizens from unsafe foreign vessels on ocean voyages, and required that vessels be made of steel; the *Queen*'s superstructure is of wood.

One might not feel safe cruising the ocean in a wooden vessel, but on inland waters the *Queen* inspires confidence. She is never more than half a mile from land and has never had a serious accident, fire, or other mishap. In an emergency, the helmsman can easily have her ashore, bow in, and gangway down, in less than five minutes.

It seemed so unreasonable to apply laws governing ocean vessels to the *Delta Queen* that a series of legislative battles were launched to save her. Spurred on by indignant citizens' protests and formal requests from numerous groups interested in the preservation of our heritage, Congress passed first an amendment delaying enactment of the law, then two special acts to extend her life.

There are only two large passenger ocean vessels now flying the American flag. Soon they may be forced off the waters by foreign competition. That would leave the *Queen* as the last major overnight passenger vessel to fly the American flag. To have her stilled, not by foreign competition but by the laws of the nation whose flag she so proudly flies, would be more than ironic. It would be tragic!

Safety, as noted in the account of the jazz cruise, is stressed on the *Queen*. Passengers are briefed on life-jacket use and the location of lifeboats, and the crews are drilled on each voyage. The owners have spent more than a million dollars on improvements. The *Queen* is a safe vessel. She deserves continued life.

Here is how one passenger on the *Queen* described his feelings about the laws that threaten her future:

"Make her out of steel? How would you re-create the sumptuous varnish work, the wood carvings and turnings, out of cold steel? Can you picture a Monticello or a Mount Vernon made of steel, a Lincoln Memorial or a Mount Rushmore made of plastic?

"I am growing weary of government, in the name of public progress or public safety, destroying the niceties of the pretranquilizer generations.

"Each time my government has 'protected' me thusly, I have found that it also robbed me of part of my past, repealed a part of my youth, my memories.

"My old fishing creek has been 'improved' now, straightened out and made safe. But there are no more fish in it nor oaks overhanging it to furnish shade. And even if there were, there is a chain link fence along it to keep me out.

"The *Queen* is the last of the luxury sternwheelers on the river. Let's refrain from consigning her to the junk heap or museum tour. We, and our children, will be sorry if we do. But then it will be too late."

Acknowledgments

To New Orleanians James Henrie and Durel Black for giving nourishment to the idea for such a book;

To Betty Blake and Steve Shanesy of Greene Line Steamers for the utmost in cooperation;

To M. Stone Miller, Jr., Louisiana State University archivist, for assistance in gathering material for the chapter, "An Ancestry of Bluebloods";

To William Crais, III, whose jazz-cruise diary served as a basis for "Affair with King Jazz" and portions of the Epilogue;

To Pliny Tassin, whose vivid recollections of turn-of-the-century steamboating days provided inspiration.

RESEARCH
  Myron Tassin
  Smiley Anders
PHOTOGRAPHS
  Louisiana State University Department of Archives and Manuscripts (from the E. B. and Philip Norman Collection): Pages 14, 15, 16, 17, 18, 19, 21, 22, 24 bottom, 27 bottom, 28, 30 left, 31 right, 32, 33, 34, 35, 36 bottom, 37, 38 bottom, 39, 40, 41, 42, 43, 44.

  Greene Line Steamers: Pages 26, 29, 45, 46, 51, 52, 53, 54, 55, 56, 57, 59, 60, 62, 63, 64, 66, 67, 68, 69, 70, 71, 72, 81, 82, 84, 88, 89, 90, 92.

  Charles Franck Collection: Pages 20, 23, 24 top, 25, 26, 27 top, 30-31 centerfold, 36 top, 38 top.

  Jules L. Cahn: Pages 58, 61, 65, 76, 83, 85, 86, 87, 91, 95.